ANIMALS THAT LIVE IN ARCTIC WATERS

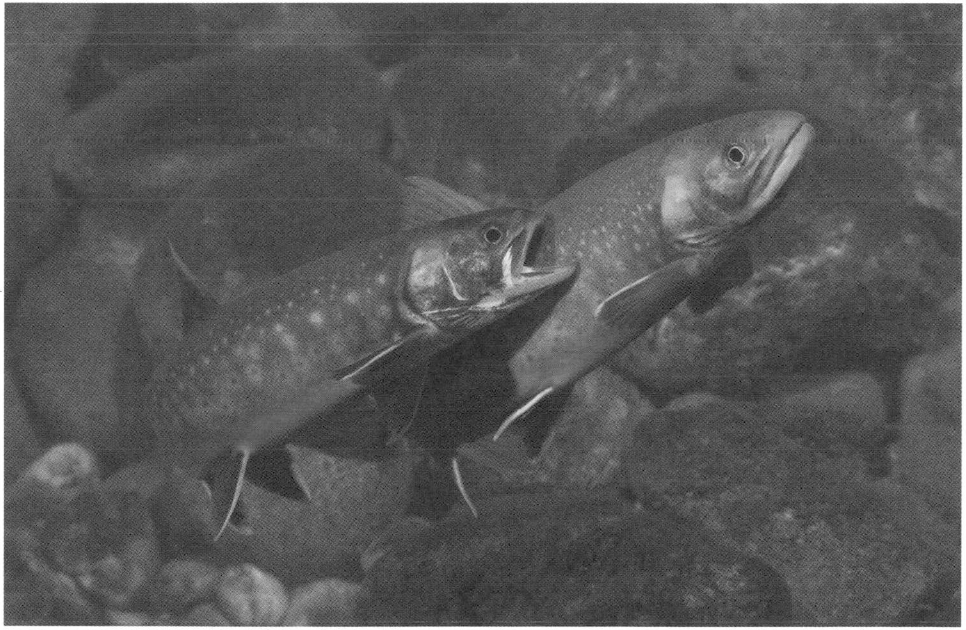

fish

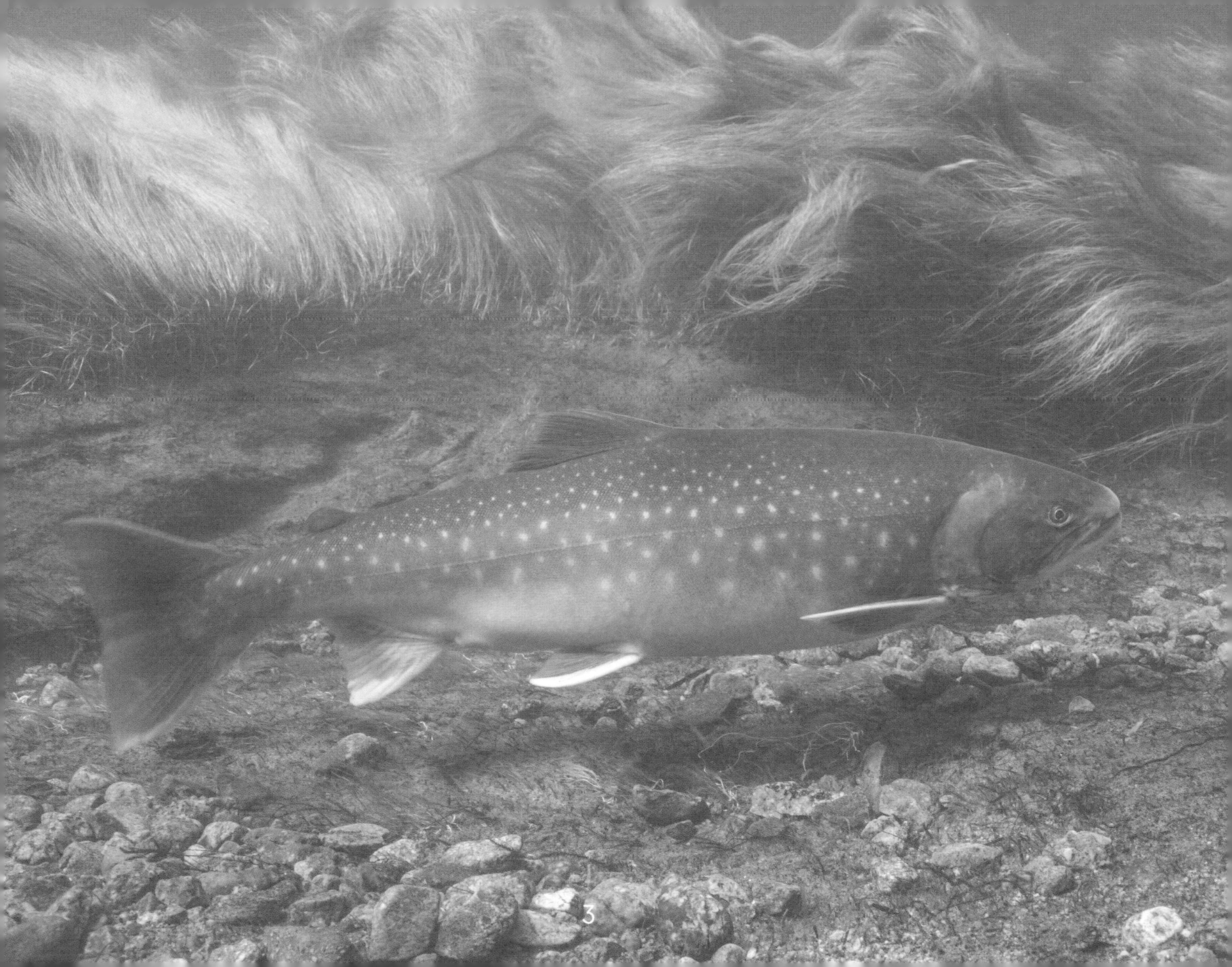

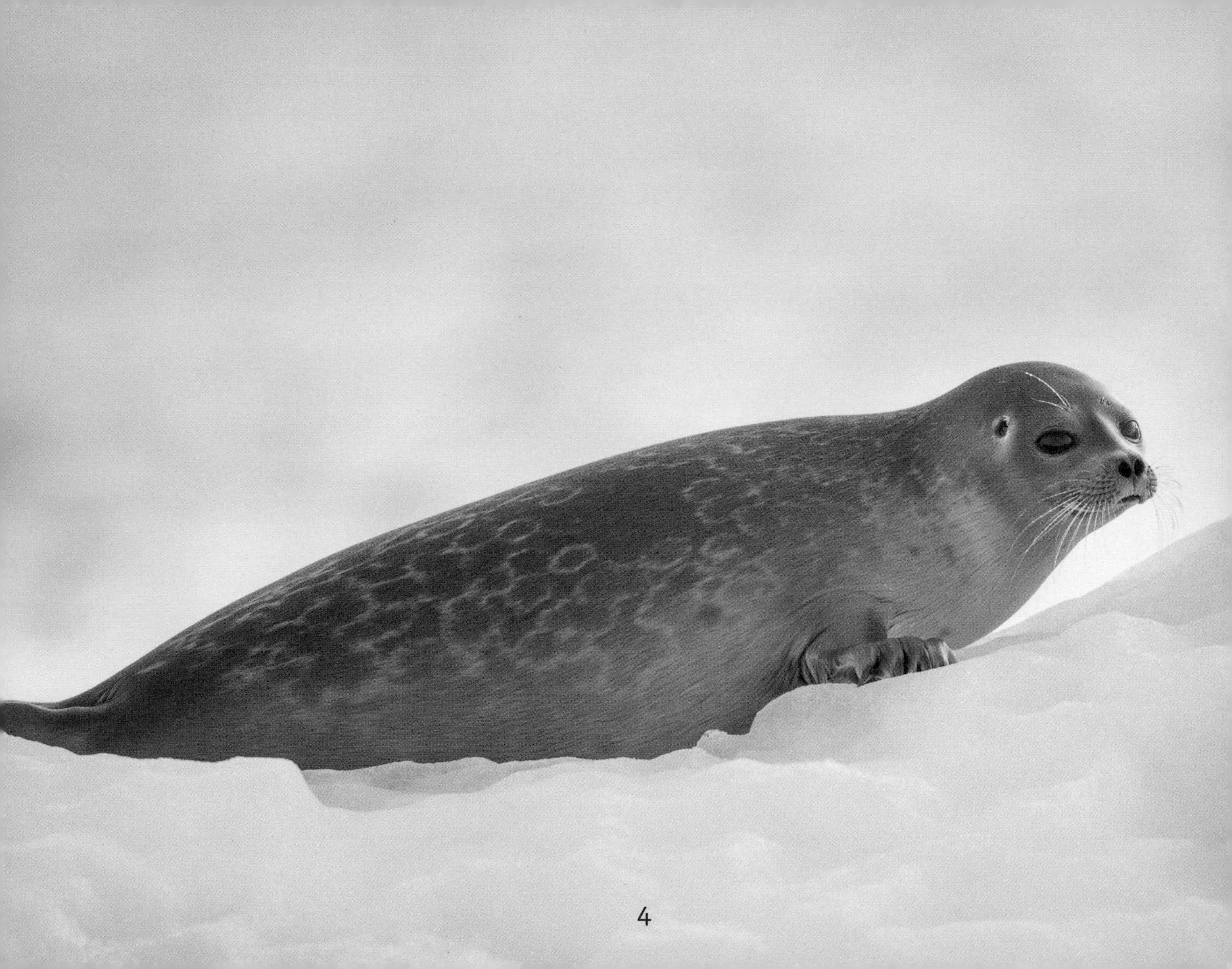

ringed seal

narwhal

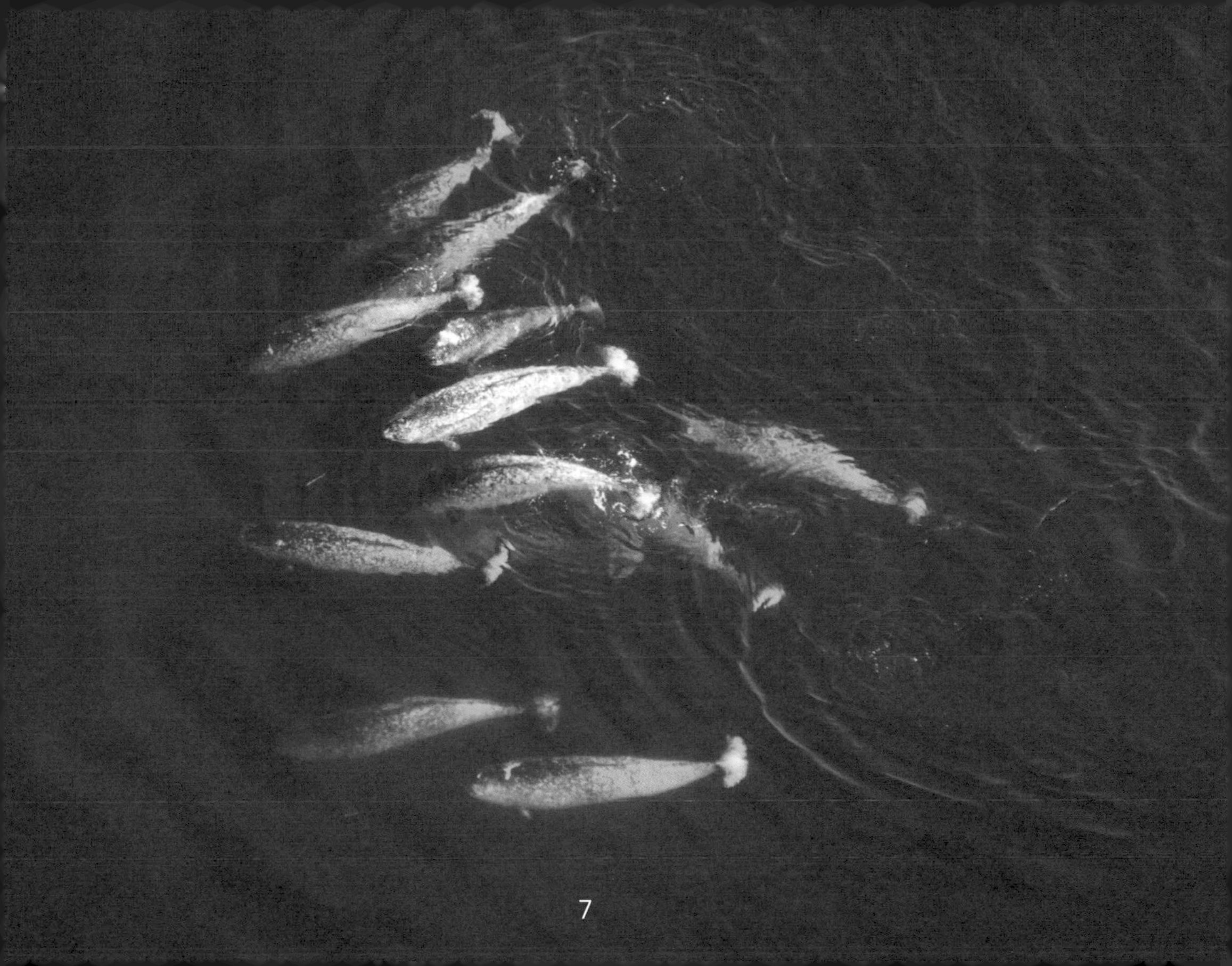

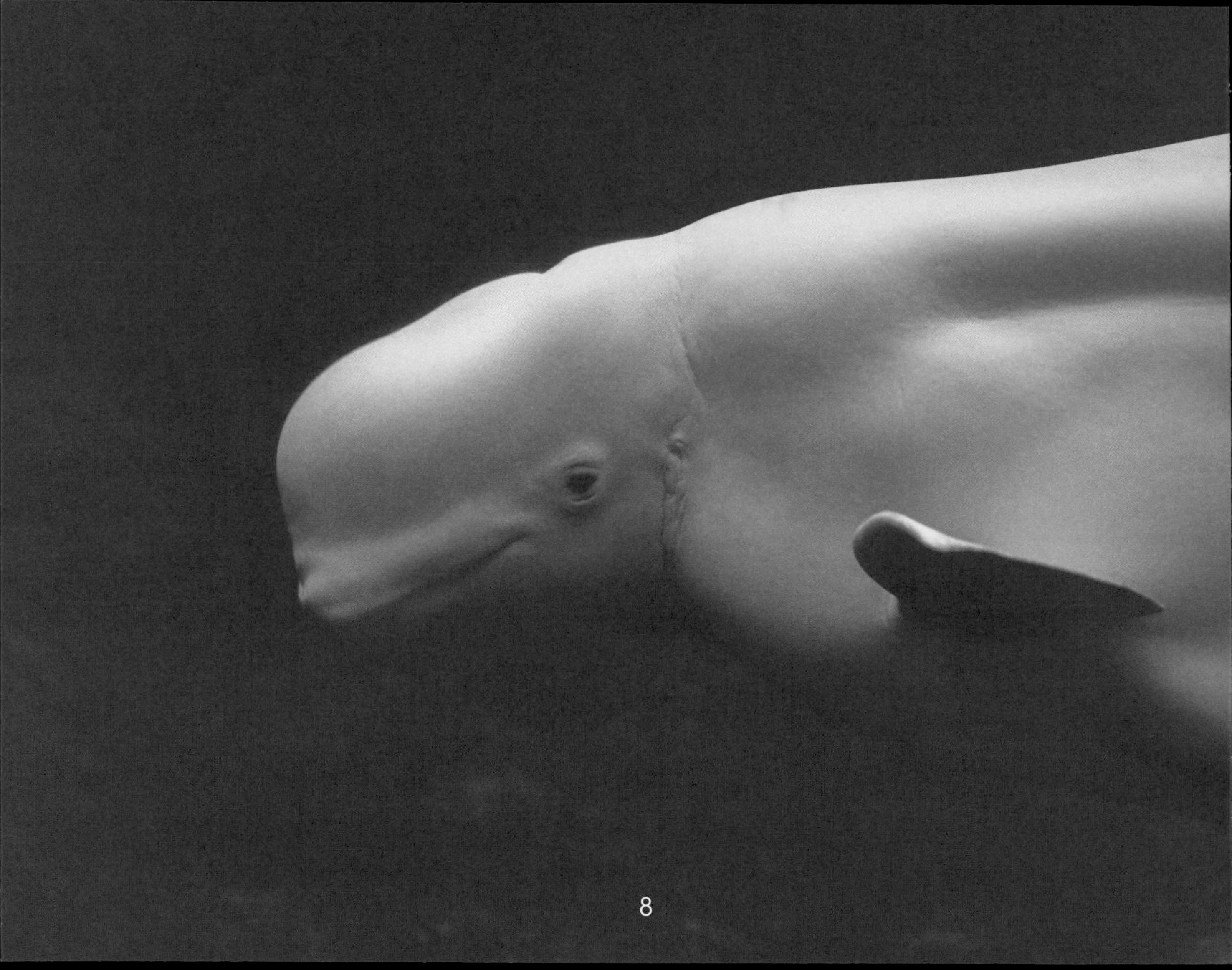

beluga

bearded seal

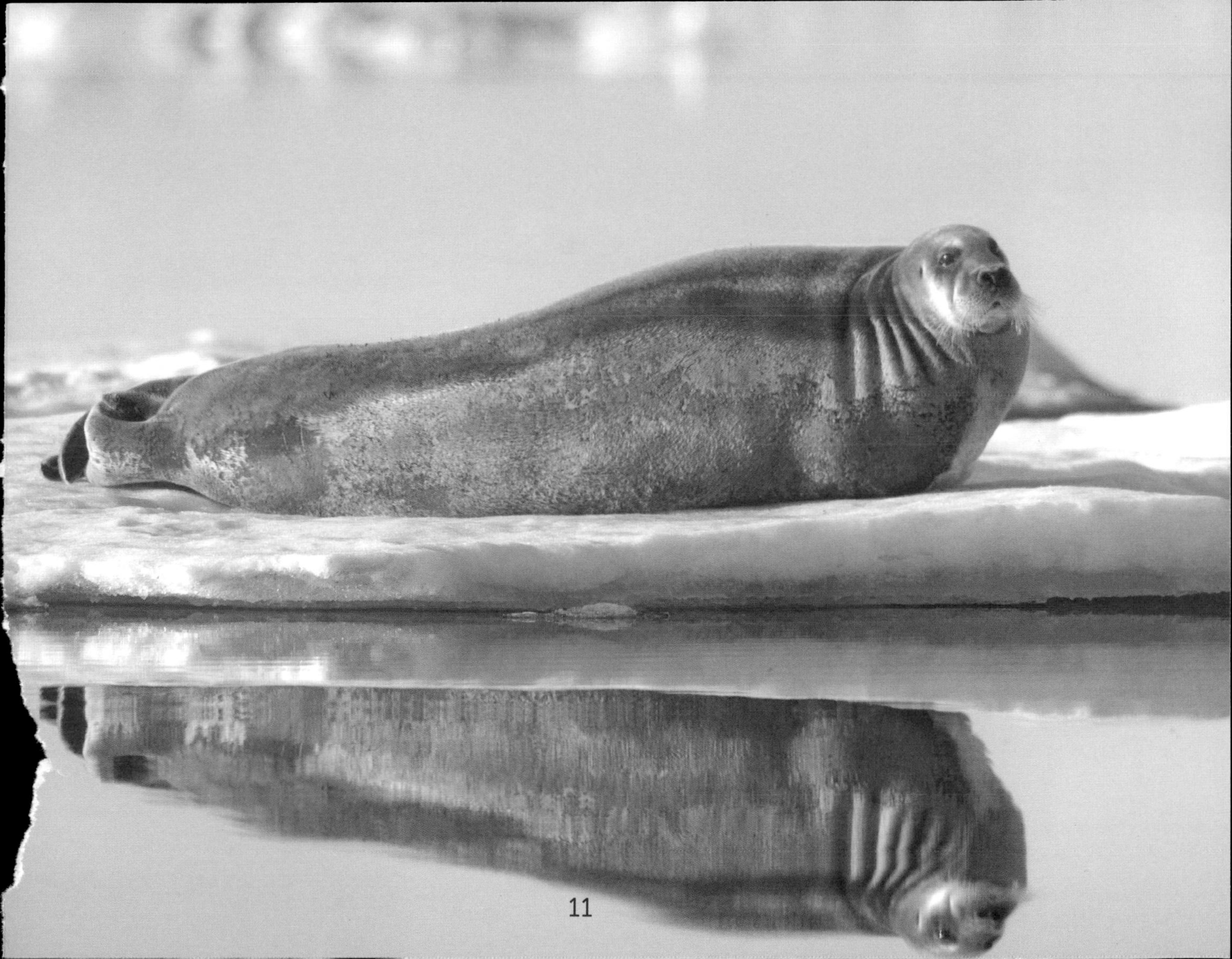

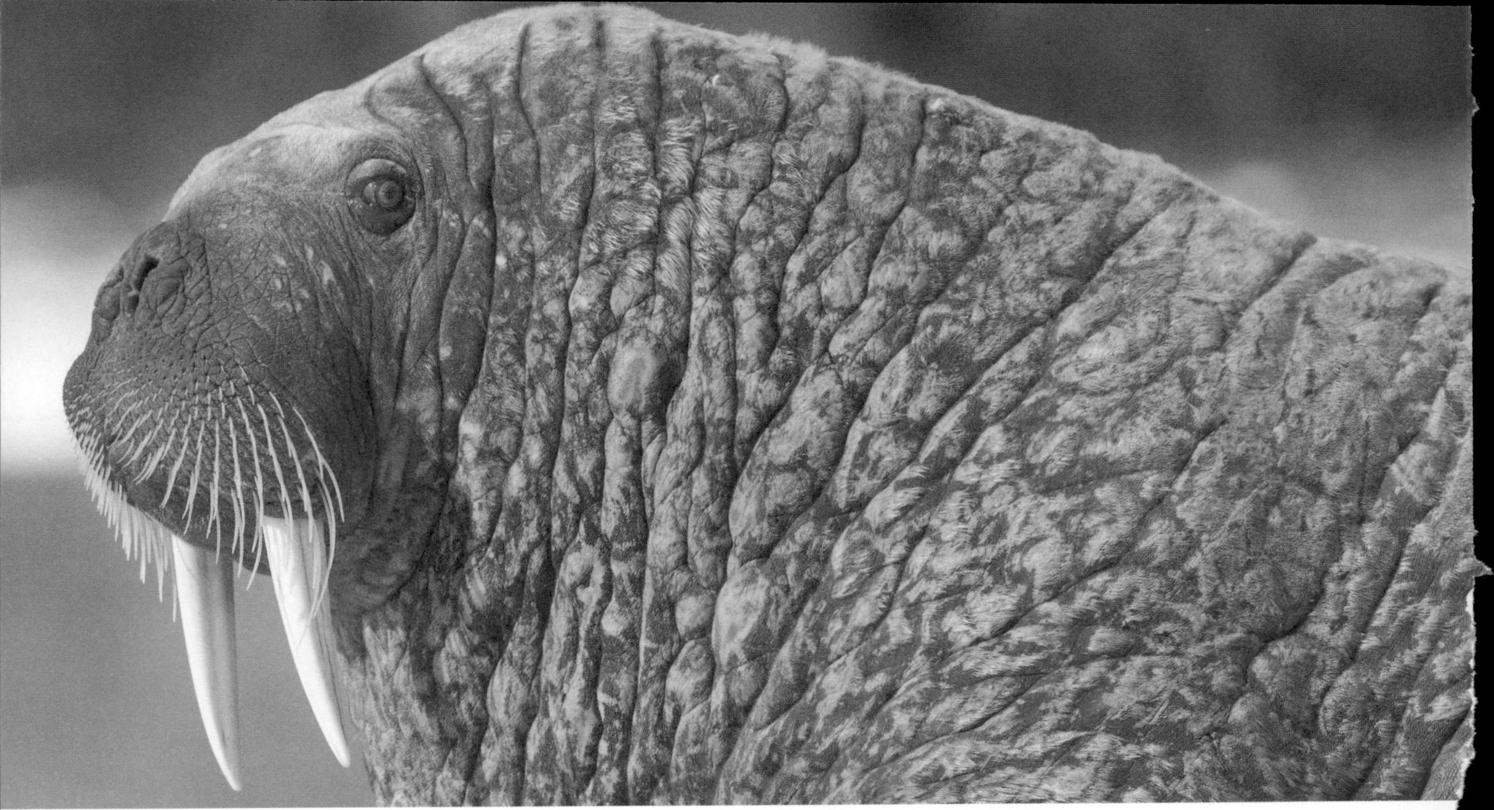

walrus